# storage style

**COUNTRY LIVING**
MAGAZINE

# storage style

## PRETTY AND PRACTICAL WAYS TO ORGANISE YOUR HOME

Lesley Porcelli

jacqui small

PAGE 1: A vintage filing cabinet fits the bill as a sideboard in a dining room. Generously sized drawers provide plenty of space for table linen, cutlery, candlesticks and other tableware. Its surface is roomy enough to hold serving dishes and to be used to set out part of the buffet. The nearly square Victorian botanical prints hung above complement the cabinet's boxy drawers, the colour combination standing out beautifully in the white room.

PAGE 2: Magazines have a way of accumulating in any room of the house, but especially in the living room. Here, a space too awkward for a bookshelf is fitted with a slim rack for magazines, making it easy to prevent them from collecting under the sofa or on the coffee table.

PAGE 6: A plate rack has been installed between two window frames, an ingenious use of space that also allows the home's original brick walls to show through. The white serving dishes and plates gleam against the textured background provided by the bricks. A saucepan rack hangs from the original tin ceiling, supporting antique copper pots and pans as well as garlic. The island unit's sides match the Shaker-style panelling that is original to the house.

First published in US in 2008 by Hearst Books
A Division of Sterling Publishing Co., Inc.
387 Park Avenue South, New York, NY 10016

First published in the UK in 2008 by Jacqui Small LLP
an imprint of Aurum Press Limited
7 Greenland Street
London NW1 0ND

Manufactured in China

ISBN 978-1-906417-13-0

10  9  8  7  6  5  4  3  2  1

# contents

# foreword

## visit a home that seems calm and clutter-free

and you'll very quickly realise the key is good storage. This doesn't just mean lots of shelves, but rather, a well-designed mix of storage – both free-standing and built-in – to suit varying requirements: open shelving for items where easy access is required, glass-fronted display areas when dust needs to be kept at bay and cupboards of different shapes and sizes so that more untidy and unattractive items can be kept out of sight.

When we include a feature on storage in the pages of *Country Living Magazine*, it's always incredibly popular with readers for the very good reason that having enough places to put things is a dilemma we all face. This stylish and useful book, *Storage Style*, was produced by our sister title *Country Living* in the US. We thought it had a lot of great ideas that we should share with you. I do hope you enjoy it and that, as a result of reading it, your home becomes a clutter-free zone.

Susy Smith
EDITOR
Country Living Magazine

7

# introduction

**whether home is** a nineteenth-century farmhouse standing on a hill, a two-up two-down terraced house on a tree-lined street or a tiny cottage at the end of a winding road, stepping through the front door when you've been away is a relief for the spirit, an escape into the privacy and comfort that we sometimes forget we need. Home is the place where we keep all our treasured possessions, but also the everyday ones; it is the place where we cook and wash ourselves and care for our families. The little details of home assume meanings that the casual visitor could never know and, ideally, they wrap us in a security blanket of contentment, endearing themselves to us as we go about our lives, every object a reminder of and a reconnection with our individuality. The worn surface of an old bread board as you slice a loaf; the feel of the living-room carpet underfoot; the beautiful patina of an heirloom dining table, and – your storage.

In an empty hallway, just one pair of kicked-off wellies and one wet umbrella would constitute disarray, but here, providing designated spaces for such items not only helps arrange them neatly, but also contributes an easy sense of style to the whole space. A cushion-topped set of cubbyholes holds shoes and baskets of sweaters, shawls, scarves and hats; a metal tray catches drips from while a coat rack extends its branches for jackets and pashminas. A fabric-covered memo board with pockets holds letters and spare keys.

If you're like most people, that word 'storage' fell like a stone, and with good reason. The cold practicality of such a concept seems to undermine the very notion of seeking comfort at home, where emotion, not practicality, rules the roost. There's nothing enticing in thinking about storage space, and as most of us feel that we have too little of it, the thought alone can overwhelm us to the point where we postpone dealing with it for as long as possible. This would be fine, except that little by little, a lack of attention to clutter eats into the edges of home's serenity – the stacks of DVDs surrounding the television, shoes and winter coats spilling from wardrobes and the kitchen units a jumble of things we don't use or even remember.

The solution is rarely found in the new generation of online or catalogue home-storage products, which intimidate all but the most enthusiastic of organisers with their strictly utilitarian bins and boxes made from wire and moulded plastic. Frankly, if you enjoyed the process of shopping there, you would probably not be seeking ideas in a book like this one. Nor does a book with the efficiency of Mary Poppins, prodding you to set up schedules and charts for purging the entire house, encourage the reluctant.

That's not the approach we're interested in here. The promise of a well-organised life will only jump-start so many people. The expected result is too vague and the upkeep too unimaginable to inspire the sacrifice of even a single precious evening or weekend to the cause.

Instead, we suggest coming to organisation through a back door, that is, viewing storage solutions in a way that makes them pleasurable, not tedious. For decades the dream homes – but more importantly, the real homes – that have appeared in *Country Living* have inspired readers with their comfortable mix of great looks and inviting, lived-in approachability, and when we looked more closely at many of these homes, we noticed clues to their welcoming style staring us in the face. In some cases, the storage tricks and organising arrangements were the very things that set the tone for a whole room, that infused the space with the personalities of the people who lived there. What you or I might put off for its sheer drudgery – say, organising the bookshelves or creating order among a china collection – these homeowners had attacked with a wit and flair that ultimately made each home unique, stylish and unforgettable.

And so, here is what we propose. Instead of looking at this book with that New-Year's-resolution sort of good intention mixed with secret dread, resolve to read it at leisure. Make yourself some tea or hot chocolate, put your feet up and let yourself delight in these pages. We suspect the most wonderful thing will happen: you'll begin to see organisation in a whole new way – not as a separate entity from the design and decoration of your home, but as an integral element of its style. And certainly, before you close the book, you'll see some ideas that will excite you enough to spur you into action. In our view, this is the simplest and most enjoyable way to approach storage, but also the most logical. After all, the best ideas for getting organised will never work if implementing them or using them is inconvenient, uncomfortable or annoying, and if they don't enhance your home.

And the same goes for the rest of your family. Of course, children resist putting things away when the task is so seemingly insurmountable – all their toys scattered across the living-room floor have to make it all the way up the stairs and into their bedrooms? An ottoman that doubles as a storage chest for their favourites will be a benefit for all – they'll love hiding their things away in this secret spot (and be more easily convinced that the excess has got to be put elsewhere) and you'll wonder how you ever lived without this easy solution. Thus, you see how the Shaker saying 'a place for everything and everything in its place' requires not superhuman discipline but a little clever planning.

In addition to this new view of storage as attractive and suitable to your life and style, we do suggest holding one concept in your mind as you read this book. Note how storage is either concealed, as in boxes, cupboards and wardrobes, or on display, as in shelving, work surfaces and tabletops, wall hangings and so forth. Why the distinction? If your clutter is the type that's not particularly aesthetic – such as DVDs, bath and cleaning products bought in bulk or out-of-season clothing – you'll want to pay particular attention to your strategies for concealment. On the other hand, if you have an overabundance of attractive things – an expansive collection of jugs, too many precious photos to stash away in a box somewhere, more books than you'd like to admit – then storage that crosses over into the display category will often prove a satisfying solution. In these pages you'll see a mix of both open and hidden storage, as well as ideas for mixing storage and display. These ideas transcend style, so they'll work whether your taste is for country chic, rustic, retro or even urban junk shop. Since the best storage doesn't look like storage, you'll notice how junk-shop bargains and household cast-offs can find a whole new useful life solving your organising problems. Moreover, you'll learn to examine all the space in your home – even that which you've taken for granted in the past – and how to play with it, how roominess affords the opportunity for display, and how furniture that does double duty, like a small chest of drawers that becomes a bedside table or a coffee table with drawers in it, will elegantly come to the rescue.

Included are lots of practical pointers, smart tips and inspiring solutions to help you organise as much or as little as you wish. We hope you'll refer to this book again and again through the years and that you will find something new every time you look through it. Enjoy.

# CHAPTER ONE living and dining rooms

## perhaps because they are the most public rooms – the first faces of your home that a guest might see

– we sometimes forget that living and dining rooms are also where everyone in the home spends time together every day. The desire to keep these rooms neat and to enjoy living in them can seem contradictory, but the intersection of these ideals can actually provide a starting point for infusing every corner with style and functionality.

Left unchecked, the clutter of daily life will naturally build up, but banishing it completely is a losing battle. The key is to keep it under control with storage that is effortless, and just as important, seamlessly integrated into the look of the room. This means, for example, an antique pine trunk that children will love rifling through to find their toys (and thus, will be less resistant to putting them away), which can double as a coffee table. In another home, a few baskets tucked under a

Two simple panelled matching cupboards constructed from recycled wood echo the lines of the fireplace and have the classic look of built-ins. Their sheer depth and solid doors enclose a large amount of storage space while maintaining the spare, easy elegance of the room. As their top surfaces visually extend the mantelpiece, they provide additional surface area to display decorative objects, with enough spacing in between them to maintain that clean aesthetic.

side table to catch magazines, books and knitting will be perfect for the job. Perhaps a tall cupboard large enough to contain a television, CD and DVD player, together with the accompanying DVDs and music, will answer the call to order in your house, or maybe simply a second sideboard will provide your burgeoning china collection with both display and storage space. Whatever the case, these rooms are about coming together with family and friends and unwinding, and you'll know that you have hit upon the right combination of style and comfort when you find yourself doing so more often.

Open storage satisfies our desire to create order and at the same time surround ourselves with things we love. This room's existing architecture offers unexpected opportunities for storage and display. Between the exposed wall studs of this informal seaside house hang shelves at varying heights, perfect for books, board games, photos and seashells, which become the central character and focal point of the space. A pine trunk topped with a cushion provides roomy storage masquerading as a window seat. A basket is also put to work for storing additional books. Despite the stripped-down décor, a few fanciful touches give the room an understated elegance: prints and art mixed with the books, a gilt mirror over the sofa and porcelain vases for dramatic flower arrangements.

AS YOU CAN INTO THE WILD BLUE.  SET ME FREE, OH

OPPOSITE: Train your eye to look for storage potential in unexpected places. Here, the backs of two old church pews were transformed into display cases and fixed to the wall. Painted white outside and black inside, they hold a set of large china serving dishes safely in place and act as display cases for the collection. The black interiors highlight the graceful shapes of the dishes.

RIGHT: Here's an example of how adding a new piece of furniture can have the effect of making a room feel bigger. This corner cupboard fits into a space that would otherwise be unused. Corner cupboards work magic for both display and storage, and the combination – upper shelves and a counter for a few treasured collectables, plus hidden storage below – is ideal for a living or dining room.

ABOVE LEFT: A dose of quirky style comes from an unlikely source – chicken wire set into the door frame of a junk-shop cupboard. But as well as the novelty of the wire itself, the openness of the piece converts the cupboard into a visual extension of the room, where a collection of gorgeous blue 1940s vases invites the eye to peek inside. Books and blankets on show and within easy reach further enhance the comfortable spirit behind such an arrangement.

BELOW LEFT: Cutlery sorted in antique sports trophies is a winning combination. The splendid patina on the latter underlines the gleam of the former, so laying the table has never been such a carefree affair. Though the dainty sugar bowl is crystal rather than metal, its double handle makes it a great team player.

OPPOSITE: Even disparate collections can look amazing together. Here, vintage clocks, sports trophies and china statues of dogs are grouped in an old-fashioned cabinet on legs, keeping them safe from prying fingers yet still on display.

ABOVE AND RIGHT: Here's a living room where plenty of comfortable living takes place. Rustic shutters front the floor-to-ceiling cupboards on either side of the fireplace, punctuating the country-style, but very chic room. Painted white, they blend with the walls, which masks their generous size. By hiding the TV and other items, they preserve the fireplace as the room's focal point. Combined with the chest-turned-coffee table, the storage possibilities are limitless. DVD and music collections, books, photo albums and games all have plenty of room.

LEFT: A modern space-saver that was unavailable to most just a decade ago – a plasma-screen television hung over the mantelpiece like a work of art – makes room for additional luxuries, in this case, bespoke bookshelves and a entire bar, complete with wine cooler, both of which provide this small room with ample storage.

# keeping clutter at bay

**it's a fact of life that the more traffic** that passes through a space, the more accumulation naturally builds. In order to battle clutter in any room of the house, it helps to think about the reasons why it's there – and there are several.

Clutter is caused by postponing decisions. If you can't decide what action to take with a letter that's just arrived in the post, for example, it is often added to a 'to do' stack that can sit for weeks. When something new enters the house, select a home for it right away and put it there diligently.

If you have trouble putting something away in its designated home, say, the food processor in a high wall cupboard, it is probably because it is not a particularly well-suited spot for it. If you use your food processor several times a week, it's probably very tedious to get out the stepladder and put it away on a high shelf so often. That makes it a candidate for a more accessible cupboard or for being left out permanently on the work surface.

You may have one system working when you actually need two. Divide storage systems into 'present' and 'long-term' or 'out-of-season'. In the case of a coat rack, only coats, scarves and bags that are worn in the current season should be kept there; the rest should be hung in a wardrobe or put into storage trunks until the appropriate season. The same goes for all rooms of the house. In winter, put your ice-cream machine and barbecue equipment in a less accessible wall unit and keep your casserole dishes close by.

If children's toys are always underfoot in a particular room of the house, such as the living room, consider giving them a little space of their own. Assign a series of storage boxes, a toy chest or one of the lower shelves of the bookcase for the children to keep their things. It will make tidying up a lot easier for them *and* you.

Your mother always said it, and it was true, that if you devote a few minutes each day to picking things up, it will prevent little jobs from snowballing into big ones. Set aside a few minutes at the end of each session at your desk or in the kitchen to tidy up and get ready for the next time.

Though this room appears casual, a strict colour scheme allows its ample shelving to become a defining element of its great style. Open at the back to showcase the orange walls, the white shelves are an excellent example of how to combine hardworking storage with display space for personal treasures. Photos, books and accessories are artfully arranged with storage boxes and baskets. A weathered white folding table also goes well, its surface generous enough to accommodate more display.

OPPOSITE: A hand-painted antique trunk is so handsome as a side table that you barely notice the fact that it offers roomy storage. Spare blankets, toys or family photo albums can be stored here yet be easily accessed. Firewood is stored in a sturdy basket.

## CLASSIC COUNTRY

Baskets have an inherent warmth and have long been a staple of country-style storage. They can stand alone or be tucked under tables and beds, or even mixed among books and other items on shelves.

RIGHT: Don't write off baskets as suitable only for the more casual rooms of your house. The clean lines of these woven boxes make them sophisticated enough for this formal interior, as they virtually become part of the furnishings. Here, they serve as filing cabinets, converting otherwise unused space under a side table into attractive and useful storage.

# 5 great ideas
# from this room

**1** Custom-built shelving divided into cubes by regularly spaced uprights mimics the ceiling's exposed white beams.

**2** The multiple shelves provide ample room to mix storage and display. Framed prints, vases and mementos are mixed with magazine files, baskets and boxes.

**3** White magazine files crisply echo the white shelves.

**4** An alcove that is large enough to accommodate a desk was incorporated into the design of the shelves.

**5** Small containers – a mix of magazine files, baskets, boxes and jugs – provide storage for periodicals, stationery and painting and office supplies. The result is a pleasing, layered mix of objects.

OPPOSITE: Though similar in theory to a bookshelf, this unit of cubbyholes invites a more playful mix of books and display objects. Vintage toys and a casual arrangement of Americana reflect the primary colour scheme of the living room, allowing the more subtle colours of the book spines to blend in demurely.

OPPOSITE: A well-worn bench painted ebony provides high contrast in this white, sun-drenched room and serves as an improvised bookshelf that doesn't obstruct the windows. In addition to providing a home for treasured books, the scale and colours of this pleasing arrangement visually anchor one side of the room.

## Reinvent It

A stepped plant shelf can be given a fresh coat of paint and transformed into a bookshelf. Binoculars and their leather case, both attractive enough to display, mix with the books to add a lovely texture to the arrangement, as does the topping of fresh hydrangeas in a silver cup.

A gorgeous mix of storage and display. The enormous antique library display cases, bought at auction for a song, are quite at home here, complementing the extra-long dining table (made from an old reclaimed door, mounted on newel posts and topped with glass) and the spacious dining room. The oversized scale of the cases provides a dramatic backdrop for an extensive collection of creamy white and floral china. The doors on the lower portion are lined with curtains, so that more utilitarian pieces can be stored out of sight.

31

OPPOSITE: An avid collector with a limited amount of space, the owner of this home turned to two classics for storage solutions. The old white armoire hides the television set and showcases a collection of creamy white pottery, while a stack of retro suitcases stores table linen and sheets. Contributing to the sense of order despite the large number of objects is the way each grouping is positioned by size, creating little pockets of symmetry in the deliberately asymmetrical arrangement of the space.

RIGHT: It's all right to crowd your display cabinet. When everything in it and even the room itself are of the same hue, large groupings can never seem in disarray. In shades of white, this collection of 1930s and 1940s pottery, together with compatible pieces found during the past ten years, is a serene work of art. Glass doors protect the collection from dust and breakage.

OPPOSITE: A collection of pressed leaves, framed and hung in a grid, mimics the grid of the old shop-fitting drawer unit. The drawers make an ideal organizer for pens, pencils, stationery or hobby requisites, and the piece is placed on top of a bench to achieve a comfortable height. There's also space underneath the bench for storage – in this case, a basket. Books stacked on top act as pedestals for a collection of antique green-glazed pottery.

**LOOK ABOVE AND BELOW** The space above a wardrobe or under a bench or side table is often the perfect spot to tuck a basket or old suitcase, adding instant storage to an otherwise unused space.

ABOVE: Painted boxes and blanket chests were commonly used before cupboards became popular and were often elaborately decorated pieces of furniture, perhaps because they were meant to safeguard personal treasures. These chests provide capacious storage and are often family heirlooms, handed down from one generation to the next.

RIGHT: Retro suitcases hold old school reports, photos and a variety of other paper memorabilia. Each case has a label indicating the contents, which makes items easy to find. By placing the suitcases on the lower shelf of a side table, normally overlooked space is put to good use. Suitcases make terrific long-term storage.

# working with professional organisers

**think of the most cluttered room of your house.** Now imagine a stranger coming in and giving that room a complete makeover, helping you to get rid of things you no longer need and finding logical homes for the things you do. It may sound like a fantasy, but this is exactly what a professional organiser does. But in case the thought of all that organising sound cold and impersonal, or inspires a vision of unattractive plastic containers, take heart. Most professional organisers agree that the idea that everyone who works with them will have to buy lots of plastic boxes or accept a new, superhuman discipline to stay neat, is completely false. Instead, organisers come up with a system that's right for you and your style, and the system should keep working long after the organiser has gone.

The best way to find a professional organiser is through word of mouth. You can also search for one online, but do ask for references before you hire anyone and be sure to follow those references up. Don't tidy up or do anything at all to prepare for the professional organiser's visit – they need to see exactly how you've been living and working. But do bear in mind what goals you would like to achieve, whether that's an easier-to-navigate kitchen, an archive system for a special collection or a clutter-free desktop.

An organiser will typically make a preliminary visit to your home to get an idea of the job and discuss the time it will take and how much it will cost. Some will charge for this initial visit and some will not, so enquire in advance. Organisers will ask what seem like very personal questions, but they're not being nosy: they just want to learn about your organisational habits (or lack thereof). Be prepared to discuss what kind of results you hope to get out of their services. And bear in mind that the relationship with an organiser will be a very personal one – after all, you'll be rummaging through your belongings together – so good chemistry is key. Don't hire any organiser, no matter how good his or her references, if you can't imagine having a relaxed, confident working relationship with that person.

You might not be able to make sense of all your possessions, but it's exactly their objectivity as outside observers that will allow professional organisers to identify the problems clearly. Organisers can pinpoint where there's a lack of storage and whether or not more storage is a possibility. They will also help you work out how to use the storage most efficiently. What about the dreaded process of getting rid of stuff? A good professional organiser will not force you to discard anything you don't want to. They'll ask when was the last time you used an item? Is the item still useful and in good working condition? Is it something you love? Is there a logical place for it somewhere in the home? And finally, rest assured that the best organisational makeovers aren't about teaching you tedious new tricks. If an organiser has done the job well, the system will be something you can easily stick to.

When you don't have space for a separate living room and TV room, and you want to keep the television out of sight when guests come, a large freestanding cupboard can hide it all away. This one is big enough to conceal an entire entertainment centre – and it contributes to the room's streamlined effect. A rough-hewn barrel in the same honey colour unifies the look – and holds a beautiful display of firewood.

OPPOSITE: A worn white cupboard found in a junk shop brings an unexpected charm to this whitewashed living room. With the door closed, the space is a pleasant sitting room. With it open, it becomes the home's entertainment centre. A large coffee table suits the overstuffed sofas and provides more surface for display.

RIGHT: Built-in shelving is always welcome. A library of books captures our imagination and their varied sizes and colours create eye-catching displays. These volumes – a collection of design and gardening books – have been stacked on their sides, creating a clean overall presentation. This is an excellent way to store antique and large-format books; storing them flat helps preserve their spines.

BELOW: Fireplace accessories are sometimes made from objects never intended for that use. Here, a sturdy old colander with the patina of age holds extra logs. Though a small touch, its very subtlety lends a great deal of style.

**MEASURE FIRST** Before building bookshelves, be sure to estimate how much space you'll need to hold your collection. For eight to ten average-sized hardcover books, such as novels, or six to eight large hardcovers, such as reference works, allow about 30 centimetres of shelving. Adjust the numbers slightly for especially thin or thick volumes.

# CHAPTER TWO kitchens

## perhaps more
than any other room, the kitchen inspires dreams of perfection. You might not have considered what your ideal bedroom would look like, but chances are you've got at least a few strong opinions about what for many is the heart of the home, the command centre of family life and the place for many evenings of entertaining. Maybe it's time to re-do your kitchen, in which case, take careful notes about what you like about it and what you want to change. Start gathering photos and swatches for inspiration, but don't dismiss the possibility of getting closer to that dream kitchen even if you are not planning a large-scale overhaul. In the kitchen, small changes can have a big impact. A slight reorganisation that takes your habits into consideration will make it a joy to put things away – maybe that unit you dip into nineteen times a day could have its doors replaced by a curtain, which, as well as providing easier access, could bring a new pattern into the space. Why not retrieve treasured collectables from the depths of the units (were they tucked

The Shaker philosophy of simple design is evident in this spacious kitchen, especially in the bespoke units. The cupboard and chest of drawers built into the corner of this kitchen provide ample room to ensure the proverbial place for everything. In addition to freeing up cupboard space, hanging a saucepan rack overhead is an especially good option when you want to draw attention to a gorgeous ceiling, like this original wooden example with exposed beams. In a room as spartan as this, what you decide to leave out on the work surface will stand out – a stainless-steel bread box and china pots holding cooking utensils keep the essentials of daily living within reach and contribute to the kitchen's character.

back there for safekeeping?) and put them on display? You'll enjoy looking at them every day, and you might even remember to use them a little more often. If your kitchen lacks character and you've always been more fond of your crockery than of your kitchen units, consider replacing your overhead storage with open shelving – a big change that costs next to nothing. And where space really is at a premium, a reframing of the question of how to store your great big bowl collection can provide the answer. Maybe it's time for the bowls themselves to become their own original sort of storage.

The advantage of open shelving is that it provides an opportunity to create a display. This enormous island unit was designed for cooking on one side and laying the table on the other. China, glassware and other kitchen items are artfully arranged with cookery books, baskets and table linen. A marriage of storage and display, the objects are so much more attractive than looking at the back of a closed unit.

**OPEN SHELVES** Open shelves work well in small kitchens because they can be tucked into corners and don't need additional space for a cupboard door to swing out.

LEFT AND OPPOSITE: Cool hues of white, stainless steel and blue give this kitchen a clean look, but it's the open shelving with china and glasses on display that lends it charm. Note how similar objects are grouped together. This turns every module into its own work of art and also makes putting things away a piece of cake. A rail above the sink is a place to hang utensils, and wire stacking shelves on the work surfaces are handy for extra bowls, dishes and glassware.

A simple solution to kitchen storage is a hanging saucepan rack. The owner of this kitchen decorated hers with enormous red crepe-paper flowers, softening its industrial feel and echoing the red saucepans. Bespoke units with glass-fronted doors show off her best china and antique ceramics. A built-in wine rack keeps favourite wines, bottled water and other drinks to hand. Everything here is useful and welcoming – even an extra peninsula unit is designed to be used as a breakfast counter or somewhere for guests to sip their drinks while the finishing touches are put to the dinner.

OPPOSITE: While renovating their home, the owners decided to simplify the kitchen and opted for an unfitted style, which was more in keeping with the country origins of the house. It's also easy to maintain. For storage, the couple selected wicker baskets that can be tucked away on shelves when not needed, or, in the case of large-scale baskets, under a work table.

ABOVE LEFT: Here's a house-warming alternative to the boring old spice rack you can buy from a department store. An old doll's house mounted on the wall is home, sweet home for all those little jars. One this small could also work nicely on a kitchen work surface.

ABOVE RIGHT: An old ladder recycled as an overhead saucepan rack brings a dose of farmhouse charm to the kitchen. Eye-bolts allow you to mount it from the ceiling with chains, cup hooks in the rails hold lightweight saucepans and utensils, while S-hooks suspended from heavy-gauge wire wrapped around the rungs hold heavier pans and colanders. But this is not a job for a decrepit old ladder – make sure the wood is still sturdy enough to hold your pots and pans before installation.

ABOVE: A compact appliance cupboard has an up-and-over door that opens to reveal the toaster tucked inside. When you've finished using the toaster, just slide it back in and close the door.

LEFT: When you imagine this kitchen stripped down to its bare bones, with only the appliances and built-in units remaining in place, you can see that every bit of its unpretentious style comes from the arrangement of the owner's possessions. Cupboard doors were removed in favour of open shelving. Each shelf has its own brand of organisation to give the overall look one of order rather than clutter. On one shelf are easy-to-find ingredients in glass jars and on another, drinking glasses. Underneath the industrial butcher's block island in the centre of the room, spare table linen and tea towels are stacked and ready for use. Aluminum dustbins are perfect for storing pet food.

Industrial doesn't have to mean devoid of personality, as seen here in the case of these two large shelf units fitted with metal baskets. Originally from a factory but bought from a specialist dealer, the shelves and baskets are just as functional as a traditional dresser. The baskets are ideal for holding groceries, cutlery and table linen – everything necessary for a well-stocked kitchen. The stacked china adds a sense of warmth. Stainless-steel shelves next to the window came from a catering supply shop. The narrow stack of lockers – a nifty storage solution that would work in a bathroom as well – was also bought from a specialist dealer and conceals cleaning products. Relatively inexpensive, the industrial items give this kitchen a delightful and wholly unexpected personality.

OPPOSITE: Brimming with junk-shop finds, this kitchen is a wonderful example of resourcefulness. All the cupboards were found at junk shops or antique shops. The mismatched lower cupboards were topped with new chunky wood work surfaces, and one was even adapted to house a dishwasher (on the far right). A vintage tablecloth acts as a skirt under the sink, hiding cleaning products or a waste bin behind it. The small shelf running across the window holds a favourite tea set that also doubles as an occasional collection of flower vases. On the work surfaces, glass jars keep baking ingredients fresh and an old-fashioned bread bin does the same for bread. Additional bread bins and cake tins stacked above the cupboards provide more storage for items that don't need to be easily accessed.

ABOVE: There is a touch of modernity in this romantic, charm-infused kitchen in the form of shelves from a catering supply company. The shelves provide more storage for canisters, teacups and a kitchen roll.

RIGHT: The charm of the wall cupboards was enhanced by fixing lacy organza napkins inside the bottom panes of the glass-fronted doors. A trio of nesting bowls add vintage charm and provide storage for fruit.

Old-fashioned plate racks safeguard and display a collection of decorated china. Plate racks are a classic country storage solution, keeping dishes at the ready and on view – a plus if you happen to own a pretty collection. The island unit's deep drawers are reminiscent of shop fittings and are a great option for storing pots and pans. Wide-necked glass jars hold an array of delights – sweets, dried fruit, biscuits and marshmallows.

57

The main room in this weekend home is divided into living, dining and cooking areas. Storage was built into the design, with the goal of keeping it simple. The galley kitchen is compact but contains an ample amount of storage. A custom-built dish rack fits perfectly into a niche between the solid-door wall units, keeping frequently used crockery immediately accessible. The long island unit has drawers for pots and pans, serving dishes and other kitchen necessities.

OPPOSITE: The extraordinary appeal of this kitchen comes from the elegant simplicity of its storage. Even the closed storage has an open feel. The glass doors allow the green ceramics to add an accent colour to the room, one that's echoed in the mint-green blender. Inspired by kitchen galley storage on a boat, a stainless-steel rail running along the bottom of the open shelf is a measure of protection against reaching for a glass and knocking others over. Below, instead of traditional floor units, are glass-fronted drawers that are deep enough to hold large pots and pans. Glass-fronted units and drawers are practical – they make it easy to find what you're looking for.

RIGHT: Kitchen units can be expensive – and difficult to plan in small kitchens because they can visually dominate the room without contributing anything extra in style. But this dainty kitchen illustrates how great style can be had on a shoestring by dispensing with traditional wall units. Exposed shelving, mounted on iron brackets and painted jade green to match the old bowls and 1930s glass, runs around the perimeter of the room. Cup hooks underneath the shelves create additional space to store mugs and teacups. Vintage swing-out towel rails above the sink are a logical solution for damp towels, and they can be folded against the wall when not in use. The lower units, painted with a light green wash and fitted with old door knobs, underscore the retro look of the shelves and glassware.

# storing fine tableware

**whether handed down from grandparents** or unearthed at junk shops, china, crystal and silverware make strong statements when left on display or presented at the table – but require careful handling to help them last for the next generation. Here are some tips for taking care of these pieces, as well as enjoying them regularly.

- Whether displaying china, crystal or silver, or storing it in a cupboard, it should be washed at least once a year. Despite their impervious looks, these materials are porous, so dust can penetrate and dull their appearance over time. To avoid streaking, dry with a lint-free cloth.

- Even in the case of tall, delicate items, such as Champagne flutes or candelabra, always store pieces the right way up. Rims and arms are always more fragile, since they weren't designed to bear weight, and laying items on their sides, even if they are well-padded, can strain and weaken them. If storing them in boxes in the attic, use padded containers and wrap each item individually. Use cardboard dividers as tall as the box so that they support the lid, should anything fall onto the box.

- When stacking precious plates or bowls, slip a round of felt or even a paper plate between them to prevent them from scratching the glaze on the dishes beneath them.

- Washing silver thoroughly and hand drying before putting it away will prevent tarnish. Do not wrap in polythene, wool or felt, as these will cause silver to tarnish more quickly. Do not store silver in a cellar, as high humidity can speed tarnishing. Do not put silver cutlery in a box or drawer where it might rattle around. Instead, invest in a wooden case, preferably lined with tarnish-resistant cloth.

- Hand washing is always best, but take care to line your sink with a rubber pad or cloth. If possible, keep the neck of the tap turned away from where you're washing to prevent scratching or breakage, and remove all rings and bracelets before handling.

Open shelving doesn't have to mean a very informal look. Dark-stained wood and a collection of fine china give this room a sophisticated air. A plate rack above the sink stores dishes, and the tiled splashback echoes the feel of the china collection. Rarely used dishes are kept high, but cups hang on low hooks.

ABOVE: An old steel industrial island unit cleans up nicely with a new wooden work surface on top and castors fitted below. As well as the work surface, drawers and cupboards gained, it also gives the kitchen great character. The rest of the room is kept rustic. A two-tiered wooden plate rack puts the china on display, while a narrow shelf above the counter adds a little more storage for a collection of favourite bowls.

RIGHT: A quirky mix of retro, rainbow and even DIY-shop chic characterises this unusual kitchen in the home of the owner of an antique shop. The unique pieces, like the old tool cabinet fitted with crystal knobs, create plenty of storage space, but many objects are included just for their aesthetic charm. An enormous garden urn is a humorous response to those ubiquitous unadorned utensil holders.

OPPOSITE: Industrial elements mix easily with wood, stone and leather in this compact but highly functional galley kitchen. A sturdy steel meat rack has been converted into a hanging saucepan rack and attached to an antique butcher's-block table, becoming the focal point of the kitchen area as well as offering storage for pots, pans and other kitchen paraphernalia. A metal container underneath holds tomatoes, keeping them at room temperature. A basket alongside on the floor is big enough to work as either a waste or recycling bin.

**MORE CUPBOARD SPACE** Hanging pots and pans from an overhead rack frees up cupboard space and provides a focal point for the kitchen.

ABOVE: A butler's pantry used to be a service room, usually placed between the kitchen and dining room. It functioned as a place to store table linen, serving dishes, glassware and additional china, and also as a staging area for formal dining and entertaining. This modern-day butler's pantry is neatly fitted with units that provide ample storage space, including drawers, cupboards and a wine cooler. With bar necessities, a sink and a dishwasher, this one serves its purpose beautifully.

LEFT: Collections stored on open shelves become the centre of attention and are easily accessed. Here, long wooden shelves that wrap around the interior of the kitchen create plenty of room for an array of vintage cake stands, jugs, dishes and bowls, showcasing the collection's many shades of white. China jugs elegantly display kitchen utensils, grouped by material (wood with wood, metal with metal). A wire milk bottle holder contains table linen and crockery. As it can be carried right to the table, laying the table has never been easier.

## QUICK CHANGE

By removing your wall units and replacing them with open shelves, you can create a budget-friendly, highly functional and casually chic new look for your kitchen. Open shelves create a focal point, as well as putting your dishes at your fingertips.

LEFT: A small pantry off the kitchen plays its part, housing a chunky wooden work surface, a microwave and a dishwasher, as well as a multi-coloured china collection that's just asking to be on display (hooks attached to wrap-around wooden moulding maximise the space). At dinner time, folding glass-paned doors hide the work space.

In lieu of pricey kitchen units, let junk-shop finds do the trick. The quirky sink unit was assembled from an old sideboard, a salvage-yard marble slab and a basic stone utility sink. Above the refrigerator, former balusters act as dividers for baking sheets, chopping boards and serving dishes. An old garden gate has been transformed into an overhead saucepan rack by suspending it from the ceiling.

If you find the casual charm of glass-fronted wall-unit doors appealing but still prefer concealed storage, opt for glass doors fitted with curtains. These wall units feature ticking-inspired striped curtains, which give them a tailored look, but other patterns, such as a floral or Provençal motif, will work, as will even a solid colour. New door handles were also added – a minor change that is quick and easy and can result in a fresh, new look.

**PICTURE PERFECT** If the interior of your food-storage cupboard will be on view, you'll want to keep the contents orderly. Put pasta, beans, flour and sugar into matching glass jars for a streamlined look.

ABOVE: Two more space-saving additions – a sliding door and a cupboard between two doorways.

ABOVE: In older homes, you may have a pantry or larder leading off the kitchen, and it can be just as charming and useful as it ever was. Connecting it to the kitchen with a door fitted with fine wire mesh opens up the kitchen a bit more than a solid door does, allows air to circulate and lets you see the contents at a glance.

Outdated wall units were replaced by inexpensive painted shelves in this classic kitchen. The shelves contribute to the room's sense of openness. The top shelf is dedicated to displaying favourite objects. Instead of replacing the two vintage lamps with a large hanging saucepan rack, the owner of this house opted to take advantage of some space near the wall on the right to install a small version.

LEFT: Replacing your cupboard doors is a terrific way to make a quick and easy change to your kitchen storage. Here, louvred cupboard doors add style and bring to mind the shutters on an old house. The nautical theme struck by the wicker and wood in white, blue and natural brown is carried to its logical end by the sheer tidiness – china is out on open shelves, but symmetry in the arrangements makes the small spaces appear neat as a pin.

OPPOSITE: Dishes can be reached in an instant in this informal kitchen in a seaside cottage. Open shelves set between wall studs hold glasses for entertaining family and friends, as well as plates, cookery books, teapots and other kitchen necessities. A skirt under the sink is ideal for concealing cleaning products and a waste bin.

BELOW: Handmade-style open shelving enhances the kitchen's airy, informal feeling – and allows plenty of space for both storage and display. It's the perfect stage for those unique pieces with pretty shapes, such as cake stands, cream jugs and bowls, to shine. On the counter, glass jars hold staples, and an elegant white dish gleams on a small shelf installed above the splashback.

ABOVE: Here, all the comforts of a modern kitchen combine with the look of an old-fashioned one. Take the dishwasher, for example, which, clad in the same wood as the units, disappears completely. There's plenty of drawer space for smaller things, thanks to the wall unit that extends all the way down to the work surface. Closing in the area in this way is not only practical, but also makes the space much cosier.

BELOW: An old bureau was fitted with a sink and reinvented as kitchen furniture. A tiled work surface and splashback complete the makeover. A sheet of wood veneer covering the original door of the dishwasher and painted the same colour as the former bureau, fits in perfectly. A plate rack holds crockery and a small shelf unit keeps glasses in order. Baskets and hooks fulfill the rest of the kitchen's storage needs.

ABOVE: If you, like the owner of this kitchen, have ever been captivated by a certain kind of collectable – say, mustard-yellow mugs and mixing bowls – you know the temptation of planning a whole kitchen around them. This can be a very positive impulse, as evidenced by the golden coat on these cabinets. The deeper shade of yellow supports the collection and creates the reason to bring out those beloved pieces from behind cupboard doors.

ABOVE: Whether frequent entertainers or parents of teenagers, you'll be pleased with the installation of a cooling drawer – a small refrigerator hidden among your kitchen units and designed for storing drinks. As well as freeing up space in the fridge, it allows guests to help themselves without having to venture into the cook's domain.

ABOVE: A gorgeous old French laundry basket mounted on castors is a beautiful match for the space beneath this work surface. Whether you use it to hold table linen or to collect recycling, the wheels ensure smooth transport to the garage or utility room.

ABOVE: A wall-mounted basket corrals handy but oddly shaped kitchen tools, like a cheese grater and cake slice. A magnetic knife rack keeps your knives all in one place and protects their blades from contact with other utensils. Underneath the work surface a thick blue curtain mounted on a sliding track conceals deep shelving that is just right for large saucepans.

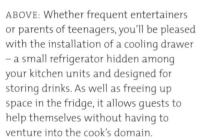

RIGHT: You can buy utensil holders in every kitchenware department, but improvising has its rewards. Throw open your cupboards and cast an eye on those beloved finds that might not get as much use as you would like – the antique copper saucepan? The vintage china jug? Or maybe even think outside the kitchen. Here, a garden urn does the job with elegance.

OPPOSITE: Updating your kitchen doesn't have to mean giving the whole room a face-lift. Remove several strategically chosen cupboard doors together with their hardware, and suddenly you've created variety in look and function. Baskets turn the spaces into improvised drawers, while the interruption in continuity gives the kitchen a new relaxed personality.

ABOVE AND RIGHT: Putting china on display in glass-fronted cupboards is often pretty enough, but the arresting use of colour in this kitchen shows how attractive cupboards can provide a backdrop for china that truly enhances its charm. An easy way to freshen up ageing cabinets is to paint the interior a different colour, which draws attention to the items displayed inside.

**EASY VISIBILITY** Glass-fronted units allow you to easily identify the contents. They also put china and glassware collections on display, but protect them from dust and accidents.

ABOVE: Utilitarian though it may be, a pantry or walk-in larder can be as attractive as any other part of the house. The key is careful organisation and a few personal touches. Much of the appeal of this charming pantry is the arrangement of the contents on its shelves. Rather than organise a riot of unattractive supermarket packaging, transfer the contents of packets of pasta, bags of flour and other staples into jars of a uniform size. Store larger items in big baskets – lining with fabric is a nice touch, as it can be easily laundered. Old cake tins, bread bins, kitchen tools and a dainty antique light all add charm.

ABOVE: A wooden china cabinet would normally be the pride of the dining room. But with a weathered white finish, it can step gracefully into any kitchen, creating instant storage. Despite its relatively small dimensions – you can tuck it right into a corner – this piece of furniture holds a great deal. Precious dishes and silver are safe behind its doors, while heavier china is grouped on top to show it off. Drawers are wide enough to accommodate plenty of silverware and table linen.

# work surfaces: what to display, what to put away

**just as you might spend hours** choosing the right tiles for the splashback or finding the perfect shade of paint for your kitchen walls, you would do well to put as much effort into considering what you should store on your kitchen work surfaces – and what you should not. These surfaces fall squarely into that hazy area between utilitarian and decorative, and generally, a mix of often-used appliances and decorative items lives here. But striking the right balance is key. Too much stuff on the counter looks cluttered and gets in the way of cooking; too little appears cold and can turn everyday tasks, like making breakfast, into drudgery.

Resist the temptation to fill your largest expanse of work surface with objects. Instead, leave it clear for working– ideally, with space for a cutting board, for rolling out pastry, for bowls to hold weighed ingredients or for a saucepan taken straight from the hob. Take advantage of awkward corners or smaller stretches of the work surface as places for appliances and display.

Arrange items on the work surface in clusters  – canisters of baking ingredients should be grouped together, as should appliances used in tandem – a toaster and the coffee machine, both used in the morning, would be most convenient if placed near each other. Transfer oils and vinegars from their large bottles into smaller containers that are better looking when left out, and store the rest in a cool, dark place.

Finally, consider the style statement you'd like to make. If all your appliances happen to be cherry red, leaving them out in a kitchen that strives for retro appeal will enhance the overall look. However, if your appliances are mismatched or unattractive, you might do better to store them away and supplement your kitchen's style with some favourite collectables – mixing bowls as a home for onions, garlic, potatoes and fruit; a display of teacups; or several much-loved jugs used as utensil holders.

Beautiful leaded-glass doors add old-fashioned elegance to this compact kitchen. Storage in the rest of the room is well-planned, too. Besides the many units, books get their own cubbyholes, and a metal plate rack both stores and displays a collection of serving dishes.

LEFT: A kitchen makeover afforded an avid cook her dream, not only in the fridge and freezer, but in the built-in bookshelves that frame them. Bookshelves can be constructed in all sorts of nooks and crannies, or they can wrap or fill any wall in the kitchen. Another creative addition is the Victorian fine wire-mesh-filled door. It opens onto the walk-in larder and graces the room with its one-of-a-kind charm.

RIGHT: This arrangement combines the sleek touches of a restaurant kitchen with the relaxed, lived-in feel of a home. China on exposed shelves provide a bit of both, as jugs on the top shelf lend their lovely lines to the room, while dishes lower down can be grabbed easily as soon as dinner's ready. Stainless-steel accessories echo the appliances and a marble work surface is gorgeous, as well as being the baker's best friend. Even when the dining hatch isn't needed for 'service', an enticing bowl of fruit will still draw the eye in its direction.

This galley kitchen is filled with storage solutions. Within one kitchen are two examples of the two-for-one: a rack installed inside the door of this under-sink unit takes advantage of its depth. A bucket and cleaning products tuck easily in the unit, while smaller items can be kept together in the rack, preventing you from having to dig around in the back for bottles and tins that go missing. In the cutlery drawer, a second sliding rack on top of the lower one doubles the space. A shallow peg rail takes advantage of the wall space.

# 5 great ideas
# from this room

**1** Salvaged cupboards from the 1920s were renovated with new marble work surfaces.

**2** An old-fashioned kitchen dresser suits the kitchen's farmhouse style perfectly.

**3** The hanging saucepan rack eliminates the need for more units to hold pots and pans and, together with the table-turned-kitchen-island unit, acts as a focal point in the room.

**4** Old church pews painted a creamy white were put to use as a showcase for serving dishes and trays.

**5** Creative storage adds fun to finding a home for the basics – an old baby crib holds a basket of fruit and vegetables.

With limited space for wall units, multiple drawers help maximize the storage in this kitchen. A plate rack keeps blue-and-white china within reach. The island unit doubles as a table, and also offers storage for cookery books and additional china. A small recess above one of the few wall units is the perfect place to display a collection of bowls, and narrow glass-fronted cupboards either side of the oven alcove hold glassware. A narrow ledge above the alcove supports a quartet of plates

# CHAPTER THREE bathrooms

## we all start our day

in the bathroom, often still only half awake, and not always ready for the day ahead. Thus, a serene setting and intuitive organisation here are crucial – a challenge since the bathroom is chock full of little things that need homes. Perhaps because we think of it as a utilitarian space, a very common under-estimation of the bathroom is to work with what's there, rather than seeing what could be possible. In this relatively small room, bringing in just one piece of furniture or one personal piece of art, can mean the difference between a haphazard room and one that looks pulled together. Instead of viewing it as a random grouping of toilet, bath and sink, cast an eye on the spaces between those fixtures. Is there a gap somewhere that doesn't really need to remain empty – in fact, that would feel a lot cosier if it were filled? Is there bare wall space where a bit more shelving would help, or even provide room for some beloved object that would make the bathroom more homely and more inviting?

A special find calls for special treatment. The owners of this Long Island beach house discovered an unusual 300-year-old marble basin from Turkey, which they had wall-mounted and fitted as a sink. An old cupboard fits perfectly underneath and provides useful storage. The sink's metal supports double as towel rails while everything else is kept sleek and spare in order to show off the antique basin to best effect.

Baskets and bins can help make sense of the smaller things. In this most pared-down of rooms, a little softness in the form of something delightfully unnecessary, just there to exist as an eye-pleaser – whether a bunch of freshly cut flowers, a beautiful print, a crystal light fitting from a junk shop or some framed family photos – can go a long way towards warming up all that tiling.

ABOVE: Twin surface-mounted sinks fitted with fabric skirts create concealed storage where none existed. The fabric skirts give you the flexibility to keep unattractive items hidden from view, while adding old-fashioned charm.

LEFT: Instead of a conventional vanity unit, which can feel too solid in the wrong setting, or a pedestal basin, which is elegant but lacks storage, the simple open shelving beneath this sink offers options galore. Supplementary shelving on the wall nearby means plenty of room for personal items. Fluffy towels and a pretty basket infuse the space with a spa atmosphere.

The owner of this home's affection for Shaker design is evident in its master bathroom. The lines of the bespoke unit are classic, providing plenty of open and closed storage for towels, toiletries and decorative items.

OPPOSITE AND RIGHT: Tucked underneath the eaves, this guest bathroom inspired creative thinking when it came to storage. An old cupboard topped with a silver tray for shaving requisites offers both storage and personality. The small corner shelf along the side of the shower provides somewhere to put soap and shampoo, while open shelving and an under-table basket make it easy for guests to find fresh towels.

## ADVANCE PLANNING

When designing a bathroom that's to be furnished with freestanding storage pieces, be sure to have all the components and their dimensions in advance before finalising the plans with your contractor. He or she will need to include any quirky pieces in the plans before beginning work.

# 5 great ideas
# from this room

**1** Antiques can be incorporated into any room of the house. Here, an old hanging cupboard reflects the owners' love of antiques and keeps an ample supply of towels to hand.

**2** New fixtures were matched to old: the vanity unit was custom-made to match the panelling on the walls.

**3** A peg rail provides a place for hanging towels and dressing gowns. Note that it's set directly above the radiator, which warms the towels on chilly mornings.

**4** Items traditionally meant for other rooms or uses can be put to work elsewhere. In this case, a rustic green picnic basket is ideal for keeping small toiletries in one place.

**5** Make-up brushes, cotton-wool balls and toothbrushes are stored in pretty containers. Any other products, especially those in unattractive containers, are kept hidden from view under the sink.

OPPOSITE: A fully upholstered bench for lounging in the bathroom is a comfortable extra but it also makes great sense when it incorporates storage. Two freestanding shelf racks under the window hold towels, toiletries and plants, while bath products in sleek bottles that maintain the colours of the bathroom are pleasing to the eye.

RIGHT: Though it's a tight spot between the chair and the window, a small antique armoire can deftly squeeze in and provide all the storage you need in a bathroom. Charmingly distressed, this one holds a little bit of everything – a television and radio (not to be touched with wet hands, of course), spare towels and some decorative pieces of china – all of which easily can be hidden away behind closed doors when not in use or when visitors drop in.

# pretty bottles and canisters

**the lovelier the bathroom,** the more glaring the bottle of shampoo with the garish label that announces, 'Now, 30% more FREE!' After putting so much effort into creating a bathroom that is beautiful, comfortable and well-organised, you don't want ugly packaging to spoil the effect. Instead, consider this little decorator's trick that might seem fussy at first, but which will make your life easier and will go a long way towards achieving great style. Decanting soaps, shampoos and other toiletries into pretty containers will make them disappear from view, conform to the bathroom's décor or contribute lively splashes of colour, depending on your preference. And in this day and age of buying in bulk, it's a practical solution as well. Opaque pump dispenser bottles in stainless steel or ceramic can be bought inexpensively in department stores or health and beauty retailers or, in a very spare bathroom that you'd like to liven up with colour, the saturated hues of many shampoos and small bars of soap will look great shining through clear glass or plastic bottles and jars. Unless your toiletries are nicely packaged, store any large or unattractive containers under the sink or in a cupboard and arrange the rest around the bath, on the counter or on open shelves. You'll be a believer as soon as you notice that it's not all those good-looking containers you see, but just a gorgeous bathroom.

Intending to create a one-of-a-kind master bathroom for her circa 1800 farmhouse, the owner set out to find components with an antique feel. She found an old mahogany-veneered chest of drawers that was structurally sound and transformed it into an elegant vanity unit with several coats of paint and a crackle-glaze finish, a marble top and two inset porcelain sinks. Shapely containers on a silver tray make elegant packaging for toiletries.

OPPOSITE: Starting from scratch offers limitless possibilities to set a one-of-a-kind tone in a bathroom. This one uses unusual utility materials – galvanised steel for both sink and bath. The wooden counter on which the washbasin stands is supported either end by chicken-wire-fronted cupboards. But as well as adding a whimsical touch, the chicken wire actually has a practical function, allowing air to circulate through the cupboards. A bathroom stool offers a place for soap and a towel. Fresh flowers and a few personal items on display ensure that this bathroom is as warm and welcoming as can be.

## Reinvent It

Antiques and collectables can adopt new roles, as is the case with these old locker-room clothes-storage baskets. Fixed to the wall, they're put to work as cubbyholes for soap, towels and even spare slippers.

### TAKE IT WITH YOU

Freestanding bathroom storage units, unlike built-ins, can go with you when you move to a new house.

ABOVE: Industrial chic, in the form of metal furniture paired with exposed brick, is at its cosy best in this attic-turned-master-suite. A vintage green metal chest of drawers sets the tone for the whole room. A medicine cabinet on castors provides a counter next to the sink, while a steel-framed mirror continues the vintage industrial theme.

LEFT: This freestanding cupboard is a replica of an early-twentieth-century medical laboratory cabinet, and keeps a basket of toiletries and clean towels on show. Its glass walls let light from the sunny window shine through, eliminating any feeling of visual clutter that a solid piece might contribute. A chair functions as an additional perch for towels or a dressing gown. Perhaps best of all, this bathroom reflects the idea that personal touches go a long way towards tying it all together – with a botanical print on the wall and a potted orchid on the edge of the bath.

ABOVE: Little luxury touches can also contribute to superb storage. Here, a silver sports trophy for make-up brushes and a miniature vase in black Wedgwood for cotton-wool balls, keep essentials shipshape in an artful way.

BELOW: Quirky details, such as old wire glove stretchers and tiny besom brooms, turn this small bathroom into one with a sense of fun. A narrow shelf under the mirror supplies additional storage space by holding silver cups that keep cotton buds, toothbrushes and other small essentials in order. Even the aspirins have been transferred to an antique glass medicine bottle with a metal cap.

## SMALL SPACE IDEA
Installing a narrow shelf beneath the bathroom mirror adds more space for pretty containers filled with cotton-wool balls, cotton buds and other essentials.

ABOVE: A lack of built-in cupboards calls for creative thinking. This bathroom was given instant glamour with a charming old armoire fronted with chicken wire, which lets the contents breathe – a big plus in a humid room – and painted a bright shade of blue. Though it's roomy enough to hold virtually all bathroom needs, the contents of the two shelves on show are arranged with extra care. Fuffy towels are stacked on the top shelf, and the attractive containers and apothecary jars for storing bathroom requisites make the middle shelf a pretty focal point.

When dealing with a tight space, think about every nook and cranny to maximize the storage space. In this bathroom, the answer to extra towel storage lay beyond its walls in the form of recessed shelving and drawers. A basket on the floor next to the bath keeps towels within reach, and, being next to the radiator, warms them on cold days.

**CONSIDER A CHEST OF DRAWERS** Any furniture, especially a chest of drawers with nice lines, that is big enough to accommodate a sink, can be adapted to make a vanity unit.

BELOW: Open shelves work in the bathroom just as well as in the kitchen. Here, they hold spare towels close at hand. An old French sideboard was stripped, painted and modified to acommodate two sinks. Bringing lovely cherished objects – fresh flower arrangements, family photos or a painting – into the bathroom draws attention away from utilitarian details, such as the chrome towel rail.

ABOVE: Even though its traditional location is over the sink, an old medicine cupboard, especially when it's a unique eye-catching one, will look perfect in another spot on the wall. Here, it not only provides additional storage for toiletries, but also functions as a work of art, injecting a big dose of character in a small space.

# junk-shop style

**there's no limit to the types of junk-shop finds** that can make organising your bathroom cupboards and bathroom counter a pleasure. Antique medicine jars, old metal or enamel medical dishes, small silver cups or china and even items from other rooms of the house – think tiny flowerpots, collectable tinware, little jugs and sugar bowls – can fit those tight spaces.

The bathroom cupboard is often the room's smallest space, but also the most important, as it's used on a daily basis. Limit its contents to toiletries, not bathroom cleaners. This is also not the place for anything used less frequently than once a week. Decant liquids, such as mouthwash or body lotion, from large containers into smaller, lidded jars or antique bottles. Transfer small quantities of cotton-wool balls or cotton buds into teacups, diminutive vases or glasses, and store the rest under the sink in its original packaging. Every few weeks, refill all the containers and remove anything that has ended up here but is not part of your daily or weekly routines.

Cupboards can benefit from planning and editing, too. Group like with like, keeping all your make-up together in one place, all medicines in another; ideally, each will have its own shelf or drawer. Small baskets can make these spaces easier to use, as can converting high shelves into drawers you can pull out or dividing large spaces into more manageable ones. Under the sink, group all cleaning products together and bulk-buy packages together, arranging them in low, wide containers or trays that keep them upright and are easy to pull out and locate what you are looking for.

Finally, consider what you'll keep on the counter. Though these items can certainly be utilitarian, for instance, if you like to keep your make-up brushes or moisturiser to hand, bear in mind that they will contribute to the look of the room, so choose containers accordingly and transfer soaps and other products from their packaging to pretty bottles and trays.

Four charming and easy-to-implement storage ideas infuse this old-fashioned bathroom (note the separate antique hot and cold taps) with all modern comforts without succumbing to any of the latest fads. A slender shelf topping the wall panelling is perfect for toiletries, candles and two shapely jugs. An antique wall-mounted medicine cupboard is just as spacious as any bought from a bathroom supplier. Ticking toiletry bags suspended from a peg rail add timeless charm, while an old enamelled flower bucket is ideal for long-handled back brushes.

Timeless materials such as marble and wood give this spacious master bathroom its opulence, but useful storage keeps it anchored in practicality as well. A cupboard and open shelf above the toilet store fluffy white towels and other necessities, while four white wooden shelves at one end of the bath hold old glass apothecary jars and bottles filled with scented soaps and colourful bubble bath.

### PRETTY SOAP STORAGE
Bath soaps stored in an attractive, open container make a lovely bathroom centrepiece and can subtly scent the room.

This vision in white illustrates
how utility and beauty can be one and
the same, especially when you have the
luxury of bespoke storage in a large
bathroom. Built-in open shelving with an
elegant arched top provides ample space
for storing towels, while baskets keep
smaller items together, including a wire
basket for loofahs. Such spaciousness
allows you to create order and a visually
appealing display, thus towels can be
interspersed with other objects that are
simply pleasing to the eye. Throw your
dressing gown over the rocking chair or
place your towel on its seat while you
bathe – when required, it stands in for a
hook. The overall effect is charming, but
even better, convenient, as all your needs
are effortlessly taken care of.

OPPOSITE: This luxurious arrangement shows why it pays to venture outside the bath department when shopping for bathroom furniture. A dresser loses its dining-room associations when filled with towels, and in fact, it balances the modern elements – the glassed-in shower and deep bath across the room. The mix of visible shelving above and cupboards below seems to make just as much sense in the bathroom as it does in the dining room and, as in the dining room, keep your lovely items on the upper shelves, and store the unattractive ones behind closed doors.

BELOW: The question of where to put towels is answered with pure luxury. A spa-inspired bathroom, sleek and modern down to its teak bathmat, wouldn't be complete without these warming drawers for keeping towels and dressing gowns toasty warm. If you're re-doing your bathroom and would like to implement this idea, be sure to look for warming drawers specifically intended for the bathroom.

ABOVE: Clean lines give this modern bathroom a fresh, airy feel, but less apparent, its ample storage space contributes both serenity and order. A roomy vanity unit with flush doors and drawers provides plenty of storage space for cleaning products and toilet paper. The three drawers accommodate all the daily needs – cosmetics and soaps, medicines and a hair-dryer. And for those items you always want within easy reach, a rustic bench next to the shower serves as a repository for spare towels, while a wire basket on the bench holds the flannels. Better still, the bench creates storage space beneath it, where baskets conceal additional toiletries.

# CHAPTER FOUR bedrooms

## talking about storage and the bedroom in the same breath initially seems contradictory: the former feels like a chore, while the latter is ideally a deeply personal, restful haven. Yet having a place for everything is the key to achieving a truly relaxing and stylish bedroom. Bear in mind that one idea doesn't fit all – a deep wardrobe may feel heaven-sent in your room, but might be unsuitable for a young child, who'd be better off with a series of low baskets that he'll love to fill with his toys. Tailoring bedroom furniture to each inhabitant's needs is what will ultimately personalise these rooms. Don't overlook the guest room – several empty drawers, easy access to some spare blankets and a few charming details that convey the style of the host are essential. It's not about keeping up appearances for those who visit, but about making each room more livable for the person who spends time in it, whether that's for just a few days or every night.

A bed without a footboard provides the opportunity to create your own visual anchor for the end of the bed. Here, it's two stacked baskets with scalloped cotton linings that can hold anything from magazines to slippers.

ABOVE: Rather than add another chest of drawers to an already full room, a collection of old suitcases and dome-topped trunks, unified in look by their distressed leather and weathered hardware, can be a much more interesting choice. Stacked from largest to smallest, they are visually appealing and incredibly useful – these can handle a whole wardrobe of out-of-season clothing or extra blankets.

RIGHT: Most old homes were constructed with very little built-in storage, especially in the bedroom. In this old farmhouse bedroom, a roomy cherrywood tallboy offers a good solution for storing clothes, bed linen and an extra blanket or two. Above the tallboy, a set of hat boxes is both stylish and practical.

LEFT: In a cosy nook of the bedroom with a chair and footstool for reading or napping, you barely notice the practical – a stack of old suitcases that not only provides a place to rest your book or a cup of tea, but is also as spacious inside as a small chest of drawers.

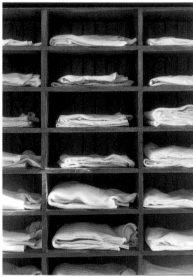

ABOVE: A place for everything, including a much-loved collection of ribbed sweaters. This old oak wardrobe was rescued from a church crypt. Fitted out with shelves, it's the perfect place for clothing that needs to be stored flat. What is more, it makes an appealing visual display as well.

## Reinvent It

Find creative uses for objects. Here, an old gardening tool hangs on a door and holds a mass of pretty necklaces.

RIGHT: This bespoke recessed unit is both space-saving and incorporates the type of drawer and cupboard combination that makes dressers so versatile. The upper cupboards can hold bags, sweaters or even a television, or they can be fitted with a rail to accommodate hanging jackets and shirts. The lower drawers, which increase in size nearer the floor, make organising your clothing as easy as pie.

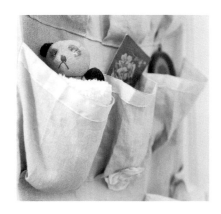

ABOVE AND RIGHT: Ignore the intended purpose of a shoe organiser and put it to use for other storage. Sewn from linen and trimmed with old ribbon, this one is filled with mementos and is a comforting presence every time the cupboard door is opened. Shoe organisers are also ideal for storing belts, scarves, hair accessories, socks and countless other small items. The floor-length tablecloth is a perfect cover for items stored underneath it.

OPPOSITE: A peg rail is a smart addition to a bedroom, as there's always a place to hang a dressing gown or a coat. But it also converts a hat collection into a characterful decorative element. Old suitcases – stylish storage themselves – complement the look.

## TUCK UNDERNEATH
Beds house one of the most overlooked sources of hidden storage – the space underneath. Under-bed storage keeps belongings neatly out of sight.

# the versatility of old armoires

**if you've noticed a recurring theme** in this book, it could be the use of old armoires. Originally designed for holding weapons and fashioned with beautiful lines and traditional craftsmanship, antique armoires can be found at just about all types of antique shops, junk shops and flea markets. Since they were very popular as wardrobes when built-in cupboards were rare, many older armoires will have a compartment fitted with a rail for hanging clothing. Adding shelving or drawers can update them for modern use. Armoires of all sizes can solve storage problems in almost any room of the house:

**in the bedroom:** Armoires still work beautifully as clothing or linen cupboards, or they can store a television, DVD and CD player.

**in the kitchen:** Use one like a dresser to house china. Those with glass-fronted doors will show off a collection, while solid doors will conceal.

**in the bathroom:** An armoire can be used as an all-in-one towel and toiletry storage zone.

**in the office:** Fit shelves with baskets to make an armoire into a pretty filing cabinet. Convert the armoire itself into an office by extending one shelf with a foldaway shelf to act as a desk.

**in the living room or television room:** The armoire can conceal an entire entertainment system. Drill holes in the back to provide ventilation and to thread cables through.

As any collector knows, storing old quilts can be tricky: While their bulk usually demands that they be spread throughout various cupboards in the house, this huge armoire shows the lovely effect of keeping them together in one place. With their folds facing outwards, they form a visual filing system – you can find just the one you're looking for at a single glance.

BELOW AND RIGHT: The master bedroom in this 84-square-metre home (formerly a school) lacked space for any freestanding storage, but the owners were able to turn this negative into a positive and maximise every bit of the small room by designing built-in storage in the awkward spaces under the eaves. The low-pitched roof created a seemingly unusable metre-high gap on either side of the room. A carpenter was hired to fill one side with bookshelves and the other with cupboards and drawers to compensate for the lack of wardrobe space.

ABOVE: Two gorgeous stacked trunks store bed linen and serve as a bedside table. Their soothing shades of brown fool the eye – these trunks are much larger than the average bedside table, yet you don't perceive their great size, as they blend with the rest of the room.

ABOVE: For a girl who loves to dress up, this vintage haberdashery-shop unit organises her collection of accessories and other treasures. Labels ensure things are easy to find. On the wall, a shelf supports a decorative collection of lettering and an improvised clothes-peg photo holder displays snapshots or small works of art.

# 5 great ideas from this wardrobe

**1** A model of efficiency, this custom-designed wardrobe does double duty – the other side functions as a headboard for the bed.

**2** Pull-out wooden trays keep smaller items such as socks, ties and pants in order and gathered together.

**3** Deep drawers give the wardrobe a solid foundation visually and hold t-shirts, sweaters, sportswear and other bulky clothes.

**4** A distinctive touch – the antique drawer handles are stamped '1786'.

**5** A shelf installed directly beneath the hanging rail of the wardrobe provides a second tier for shoe storage.

ABOVE: Little cubbyholes have a cosy appeal and work for children of all ages. Younger children love turning each section into a sort of diorama with their toys, while older ones will appreciate having their favourite things to hand.

LEFT: A collection of Bakelite horse brooches, old Navajo and Mexican silver and a bevy of new and vintage belts play up the Wild West theme in this home. While one belt or brooch may not catch the eye, when displayed together, their appeal is amplified. The crude construction of the display case and its straightforward approach to keeping objects in order appealed to the owner's sense of practicality.

Many people don't invest much in the aesthetics of their wardrobes since the space is not on display. We prefer the sensibility of this couple's walk-in wardrobe. Knowing that attractive surroundings feel more orderly and pleasant, they put effort and a sense of fun in every corner. Stenciling the walls with 'his' and 'hers' spells out whose belongings go where, and note the impact of the wallpaper in what is generally a drab space. Invest in the finest shelving you can afford, because solid, quality shelving is worth its cost both in good looks and ease of maintenance. Boxes and bins function as drawers to customise the shelving even further.

# the interior of a walk-in wardrobe

## every space in the house should feel good to you, including the wardrobe.

Customising a walk-in wardrobe's hanging rails, drawers, shelves and cubbyholes to suit your needs can make it feel as if you have doubled your storage space, but paying attention to the aesthetics of the wardrobe will actually help it stay organised and easy-to-use for a long time. A lot of people ignore their wardrobe or don't put much effort into its aesthetics, because wardrobes are such utilitarian spaces. Paint the inside a stimulating colour that you love, and since the clothing will hide most of it, don't be afraid to go bright. And choose a glossy finish that will resist marks from hangers and will not rub off on clothing. Alternatively, the inside of the wardrobe is an excellent candidate for wallpaper that you might hesitate to use in a more visible part of the house.

Paring down your clothes collection is a good first step to planning the interior of a wardrobe and this should be done even before you design its layout. Consider the often-stated rule that if you haven't worn something for a year, you should get rid of it (although if you really love something, you should keep it), and be disciplined about whether an item deserves space in your new wardrobe. The skirt you wear once a week? Of course, hold onto it. The one you try on once a week, then put back in the wardrobe because you don't like the way it fits? Now's the time to get rid of it.

Consider whether a standard wardrobe arrangement will work for you. With a notepad and pencil in your hand, assess the amount of space your clothing currently occupies, from outdoor clothing all the way to belts and jewellery. And don't assume that you need to double or triple your current space in order to make the project worthwhile – going a lot bigger than you actually need will allow more time to elapse between clean-outs, and the space can then feel more confusing than a small, well-edited wardrobe. Do you already have a large chest of drawers that has more than enough room for your jumpers? Then there's no need to plan wardrobe space for them. On the other hand, perhaps your handbags have never had a logical place to go: a series of cubbyholes can help keep them in order. If, like most people, your clothing consists of separates, two rows of hanging rails, one above the other, may be a better use of space than just a single rail. Be sure to include enough hanging space for long skirts, coats and evening dresses that are worn regularly. (Evening dresses that are worn very infrequently are best stored folded, rather than hung, as their weight can pull them out of shape over a period of time. Shake them out and re-fold every year to avoid permanent creases.)

Include storage for accessories, too. Small sections inside a drawer can accommodate rolled-up belts, but if you have just a few belts, then several hooks along a wall can suffice. Shoe boxes or a shelf divided into sections with uprights will help keep all your pairs organised and at the ready.

Since you've invested so much time and energy in your wardrobe, don't stop short at the hangers. Now is the time to invest in uniform, matching wooden or fabric-padded hangers. Though they may seem extravagant, they will maintain even spacing in the wardrobe, protect your clothing from stretching out of shape and prevent that frustrating tangle that can occur with a mixture of wire and plastic hangers – and they'll go a long way to making your wardrobe feel neatly organised.

# CHAPTER FIVE hard-working spaces:

## OFFICES, HALLWAYS, LANDINGS AND UTILITY ROOMS

# compared with

a newly streamlined kitchen, organising your hallway, landings, utility room or office can seem rather dull. But it's not enough to arrange your kitchen, living room, bedroom and bathroom and just hope that everything else will fall into place. Without a plan, all too often the nooks and crannies of the home are forgotten, both decoratively and otherwise, and thus they quickly become unruly. These spaces arrive at this sorry state because we often ask more of them than we do of larger rooms. These are the places where we leave our coats and shoes, where we store overspill from other parts of the house and where potentially messy chores are done. These are transitional spaces that we burden with double and sometimes triple duty – the office that doubles as a hobby room, the landing connecting the bedrooms that has become home to textbooks and backpacks, and the entrance to a home – the classic parking place for everything that comes

In a laundry room, where a good dose of cheer goes a long way, an antique doll's house mounted on the wall with ornate wooden brackets functions as storage for cleaning materials. Instead of a plain laundry bin, there is a doll's crib for folded washing, while an old table topped with a towel provides a surface for spot-cleaning and quick pressing.

through the door. Disorder here can creep quickly into the serenity of the other rooms. Luckily, even small additions made here pay big dividends. A few hooks and a table by the front door can be enough to keep all jackets, bags and shoes together; a set of bookshelves in the hallway adds layers of richness and an additional place for books and artwork. Old trunks, chests of drawers and even wardrobes might sound like surprising additions to the hallway, but they can truly enhance the look of this space, providing a visual anchor and sense of scale – and of course, lots of storage space.

LEFT: An elegant collection of oars is both safely stored and beautifully displayed in this ingenious rack. Notches in the ledge across the bottom and in the bar across the middle hold each oar in place. Perfectly displayed, their natural hues and graceful shapes accent the rustic atmosphere created by the tree trunk and the folding chair.

RIGHT: Active families need somewhere to leave their coats, fleeces, boots, sports equipment and countless other types of gear. Hooks, a table and a bench or chair are imperative in a hallway like this one, which handles a lot of dirty traffic on a daily basis. The whimsical horseshoe hooks (made by joining two horseshoes together at right angles) manage their job with style and invite good luck as well. A farmhouse table acts as a temporary resting place for items waiting to be transported elsewhere, such as these flowerpots and gardening tools. The diminutive pony can be put to use as a place to sit while removing muddy shoes or boots.

BELOW: An unexpected arrangement in the spacious creamy white hallway of this weekend house is a first invitation upon entering to shake off the conventions of the everyday. Vintage medicine cupboards provide storage for each family member's weekend necessities, as well as a place to leave post or notes. White dining chairs beneath are places to throw jackets or overnight bags, as well as somewhere to sit while lacing up shoes. Wall-mounted chairs add visual character.

ABOVE: In an extension to a historic eighteenth-century home, new owners made sure that the built-in cupboards suited the lines and materials of the original structure. In keeping with the house's American Colonial style, the cupboard doors are panelled and fitted with handsome black iron door furniture. The doors follow the slope of the roof at the rear of the house.

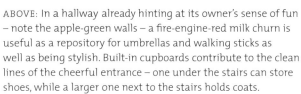

ABOVE: In a hallway already hinting at its owner's sense of fun – note the apple-green walls – a fire-engine-red milk churn is useful as a repository for umbrellas and walking sticks as well as being stylish. Built-in cupboards contribute to the clean lines of the cheerful entrance – one under the stairs can store shoes, while a larger one next to the stairs holds coats.

ABOVE: Set beneath a staircase, no space is taken for granted in this Alice-in-Wonderland-style office. Bookshelves have been cut to the angle of the overhead steps, while open modular storage has been installed under the desk. Drawers set right into the two bottom stairs will make finding a pen or pencil a task that puts a smile on your face. Though the office doors can be closed and the chair turned round to face the room when not in use, this arrangement is so appealing that you won't mind leaving it on show.

# home-office storage

## whether your desk fits into an alcove or spreads right across a roomy home office, keeping desk supplies in order can be a challenge. To make the most of this work space, analyse your options. Are there enough shelves and drawers to accommodate files and office necessities or do you need to supplement these with additional organisers? Start with the desktop, and work from there.

Think of the desktop as being like a kitchen work surface. Only keep out things that you use all the time and if you often work with paper files, get a desktop vertical file holder for those you're currently working on. If you don't, there's no reason why files should be stored on your desk at all.

Go vertical to save space: fix a memo board above your desk to hang a calendar and important notices on, such as invitations, conference announcements and reminders.

Create a spot for 'action' papers. These are things that need to be acted upon promptly, such as letters that require a quick response, bills and so forth. And if you use your office as a general work area, this applies to non-paper items as well. For instance, if you have particular bits and pieces that you're currently working with, create a spot on or in your desk where they can all be stored for neatness' sake, but also so you can always find them.

Put financial files into long-term storage every year, but keep one permanent file handy with things that you may want to locate quickly, such as marriage and birth certificates, papers relating to your property and car, passports and other documents. For extra protection, consider storing them in a fireproof safe or at least keep copies of everything somewhere other than your home, such as in a safe-deposit box.

A dining table tucked into an alcove makes a desk that's big enough to accommodate two. The bookcase mounted above lends it plenty of useful space, while the niches of varied sizes create visual interest as well. Smaller niches along the bottom are fitted with baskets that function as pull-out trays. Hung in front of the bookcase is a favourite painting, which helps integrate the whole into the style of the rest of the room and provides a lovely place to rest your eyes when working at the desk.

Create a master list of the documents that you have stored in a special place so that you don't forget what's filed where (everyone thinks they'll remember, but they never do). Make a list of these things, and keep a copy on your computer and a hard copy elsewhere, such as stuck to the inside of a kitchen unit.

No office is complete without a wastebin, which helps keep order by allowing you to throw away what you don't need immediately.

And finally, customise storage to your specific office needs. For instance, magazine files will keep magazines, catalogues and brochures neat and orderly, while bookends will hold reference books in place.

OPPOSITE: A covered porch is the boundary between the house and the outdoors, which is why both garden and indoor furniture fit in beautifully here. A great junk-shop find, the iron cage houses a collection of watering cans and garden-themed items, such as flowerpots and nesting boxes. The small bench and several decorative wall hangings complete the look.

ABOVE: Putting the results of a lifetime of collecting on display can create a unique, deeply personal effect that could never be achieved with wallpaper and decorator's tricks. This custom-built storage for model boats makes what would otherwise be a generic space into the defining décor of an upstairs landing. The rest of the landing is kept neutral with white paint and natural wood. Small splashes of nautical hues from the boats themselves are all the colour the space needs.

# 5 great ideas from this office

**1** The vintage wire locker-room baskets hold individual projects that are work in progress.

**2** A curtain rail with café curtain clips provides a gallery-like space to hang photos, postcards or inspirational ephemera.

**3** A chunky towel rail was installed to hold the bright spools of ribbon. They add a splash of vibrant colour to the work space in addition to being easy to access.

**4** Little drawer units, vintage biscuit tins, baskets and wire racks are just a few of the receptacles here that keep small items handy and add personality.

**5** A charity-shop desk was fitted with a painted plywood top that's longer than the desk. Open shelves were installed under the overhang, creating more storage space underneath.

ABOVE: An antique seed-packet display case makes a logical desk accessory for anyone planning a garden, but it has charm enough for keeping stationery organised as well. Though the desk itself only has one shallow drawer, the garden shelving has plenty of room to store all your office requirments.

LEFT: Rows of crisp white-painted shelving around the upper perimeter of this utility room turn pots and vases into an artful display. The rest of the room is similarly fitted for the gardener. Open shelving beneath the counter holds vases and baskets for gathering cuttings, while a wide, deep sink is roomy enough for flower arranging.

OPPOSITE: Verandas are an extension of the house, especially during the summer. In order to make the veranda a truly welcoming spot, you need to keep it just as clutter-free as the rest of the house. Here, a storage box on castors can hold magazines and toys and is easily tucked away out of sight when guests arrive.

ABOVE: Every car should be equipped with an emergency kit. Vintage tin picnic baskets happen to be the perfect size for all the essentials, and you can tuck them away in a back corner of your boot. Be sure to include jump leads, an emergency triangle, an air compressor to pump up your tyres from the cigarette lighter, first-aid supplies, a torch, a road map and a few bottles of water.

LEFT: A series of notches cut into shelves is a clever solution for storing wellies and keeping the floor clear. Hanging them upside down allows them to dry completely, without dripping into the boots hung beneath.

ABOVE: In a back-door hallway with a cupboard, consider a curtain instead of a cupboard door. Rainwear and muddy boots can be concealed in an instant, freeing a peg rail and a shelf, with elegant curved brackets, for garden tools and flowerpots.

LABEL IT In your enthusiasm to put away boxes and bins filled with items to be stored long term, don't forget to label the containers. When it's time to find something, you'll want to locate the correct container at a glance.

ABOVE AND RIGHT: Hard-working storage is the key to a well-organised garage. Draw on shelving, cupboards, baskets and bins to keep together all the tools, sports equipment, car parts and toys that tend to accumulate in this space. Label each box or bin so one glance will help you find what you are after. A wall of pegboard keeps screwdrivers, clamps and other tools accessible and on show. Keeping the space white imparts a crisp, clean feeling, while the red accents prevent it from looking sterile. A basket rounds up a collection of balls. There's a place for everything here, including room to tuck a small refrigerator under the work table.

# sorting through long-term storage

**when it comes to the garage, attic and cellar,** aesthetic considerations rarely come into play – we'd rather focus our efforts on the visible rooms of the house. But ignoring these spaces can make navigating them more difficult than necessary. Here are some tips for keeping these areas usable:

- Attics are prone to intense heat and cellars are prone to moisture. Store any treasured photographs and collectables that are vulnerable to the elements in bedroom or ground-floor cupboards rather than in one of these two spaces.

- Whenever you go into the attic or cellar, give all your storage a quick once-over to make sure that everything is in good condition and hasn't become damp or otherwise damaged.

- If you have a cellar, it is particularly prone to becoming a dumping ground for the whole family, so weed things out every six months.

- In the attic, do not store anything in plastic bags, which can melt in extreme heat, trap moisture and promote mould and mildew. Instead, look for tightly woven cotton garment bags to store clothing, and acid-free boxes for other keepsakes.

- Create an inventory, label and number the boxes and keep a list of their contents in a safe place.

- In a cellar, invest in a dehumidifier and keep everything off the floor on wooden pallets or shelves to protect boxes and items from water in case of flood.

- When storing anything valuable in the attic, be sure to drape it loosely with a plastic dustsheet to protect it from leaks overhead.

A former storage cabinet for nuts and bolts from an ironmonger's shop anchors the décor of this hallway, bringing a touch of informality to the casually elegant space. And since it's in the hallway, it can pick up the storage slack from any of the surrounding rooms, for instance, sewing requisites, spare lightbulbs and miscellaneous household tools.

ABOVE: Easy accessibility maximizes efficiency. Long, open shelves keep laundry necessities within easy reach. Clear jars let you see exactly how much detergent you have left. And a peg rail can hold hand towels, hangers – even a watering can – at the ready.

OPPOSITE: Just because it happens to be a place where chores are done doesn't mean a laundry room has to look dull. A wall of shelves painted apple green (and complemented with feminine floral wallpaper) functions as an extension of the linen cupboard. A collection of baskets makes sorting and transporting laundry easy, but when not in use, they convert the shelves into a makeshift chest of drawers. Even when full, they're light enough to easily pull out and lift.

ABOVE: This laundry room benefits from the roomy furniture normally used in a kitchen. A large china cupboard is ideal for storing linen, while a table provides storage space for detergents, coat hangers and ironing supplies. The generous work surface means plenty of room for folding and sorting clean laundry. A basket always comes in handy when it's time to change the bed linen, and when not in use, it beautifully finishes off the room.

OPPOSITE: At one end of an open-plan living and dining room, a wall full of built-in shelves and drawers creates a charming home office. It can be a challenge to combine an office with a public room of the house, but it works here thanks to beautiful shelving – which complements the décor of the rest of the room – and the fact that there's plenty of decorative display mixed with the practical. Shelves, drawers and baskets help sort business and pleasure, and a memo board fixed behind the main desk area carves out a place for pinning up notes.

RIGHT: Renovating a farmhouse allowed the owners to custom-design a hallway. The wide dresser stores and displays collectables, including stoneware crocks, nineteenth-century bowls, animal figures and an abundance of jugs. An early-twentieth-century American pack basket, an attractive decoration, is also handy for using on picnics. The orange-painted pine cupboard, which dates from the 1850s, keeps shoes tucked away when not in use.

**BE INSPIRED** Your home office should delight you and fill you with inspiration. Peruse books about artists' and writers' studios for ideas about decorating and organising your work space.

OPPOSITE: In a room too small for a normal-sized desk, the spindly legs of a pair of trestles maintain a light, airy feel. A tiny wooden box attached to the back of the old school chair acts as desk drawer of sorts, holding notebooks and pens. The bookshelves, filing cabinet and wall colours contribute a sense of playfulness – perfect for inspiring creativity while working.

RIGHT: Many vintage cupboards are tall and deep. Fitted with a shelf for a computer and a pull-out drawer for a keyboard, this space makes a compact office that can be folded away – a particularly good feature in a boy's room, where spontaneous chaos can occasionally erupt. Here, a memo board is mounted on the inside of the door and drawers provide ample storage for pens and paper.

OPPOSITE: In many homes, the laundry room is an afterthought, often considered nothing more than a utility room. But to make the most of your laundry room, organisation is key. Here, an alcove has been fitted with shelves and dedicated to storing clean laundry. Individual baskets make it easy to sort the clothes and linen, and each basket is labelled with a name tag so family members can quickly identify which one is theirs. Simple ticking curtains hung on a rail conceal under-sink storage with a casual, countrified effect. Store a laundry basket, waste bin or spare detergent underneath, but take care when there are children or pets around. Above the washer and tumble dryer is a wide work surface that's perfect for folding laundry. You may want to install a small television or radio to help pass the time while you're folding and ironing. A peg rail is perfect for hanging delicates or damp items to dry.

**SHAKER STYLE** Peg rails are a Shaker tradition and can be cut to fit a wall space of any size – short or long – and installed in any room of the house.

ABOVE: Winter boots and coats are the kind of thing you want to hide away. But when it's sunhats and sandals at a coastal cottage, catching sight of them in the hallway simply reinforces a sense of breezy relaxation. Here, a peg rail is a place to hang hats and beach bags, while baskets slotted between shelves can hold towels, sun-block cream, spare flip-flops and whatever else might need to be carried in and out of the house.

# Photography Credits

Page 1: Steven Randazzo
Page 2: Keith Scott Morton
Page 6: Robin Stubbert
Page 8: Andrew McCaul
Page 12: Keith Scott Morton
Pages 14–15: Dominique Vorillon
Page 16: Keith Scott Morton
Page 17: Michael Luppino
Page 18 (top): Steven Randazzo
Page 18 (bottom): Keith Scott Morton
Page 19: Keith Scott Morton
Pages 20–21: Keith Scott Morton
Page 21 (top): Keith Scott Morton
Page 21 (bottom): Keith Scott Morton
Page 22: Steven Randazzo
Page 24: Julian Wass
Page 25: William P. Steele
Page 26: Keith Scott Morton
Page 27: Gridley & Graves
Page 28: Michael Luppino
Page 29: Michael Luppino
Pages 30–31: Michael Luppino
Page 32: Steven Randazzo
Page 33: Michael Luppino
Page 34 (left): Gridley & Graves
Page 34 (right): Laura Resen
Page 35: Michael Luppino
Page 37: Keith Scott Morton
Page 38: Gridley & Graves
Page 39 (left): Steven Randazzo
Page 39 (right): Keith Scott Morton
Page 40: Keith Scott Morton
Pages 42–43: Keith Scott Morton
Page 44: Steven Randazzo
Page 45: Steven Randazzo
Pages 46–47: Jonn Coolidge
Page 47: Jonn Coolidge
Page 48: Michael Luppino

Page 49 (left): Andrew McCaul
Page 49 (right): Andrew McCaul
Pages 50–51: Grey Crawford
Page 51: Keith Scott Morton
Pages 52–53 (all): Keith Scott Morton
Pages 54–55 (all): Michael Luppino
Pages 56–57: Jeff McNamara
Page 58 (top): Laura Resen
Page 58 (bottom): Pierre Chanteau
Page 59: Jonn Coolidge
Pages 60–61: Keith Scott Morton
Page 61: Keith Scott Morton
Page 62: Keith Scott Morton
Page 63 (all): William P. Steele
Page 64: Keith Scott Morton
Page 66: Keith Scott Morton
Pages 66–67: Keith Scott Morton
Page 68: Keith Scott Morton
Page 69: Keith Scott Morton
Page 70 (top): Steven Randazzo
Page 70 (bottom): Keith Scott Morton
Page 71: Keith Scott Morton
Page 72: William P. Steele
Page 73 (left): William P. Steele
Page 73 (right): William P. Steele
Pages 74–75: William P. Steele
Page 76: Keith Scott Morton
Page 77: Dominique Vorillon
Page 78 (left): Keith Scott Morton
Page 78 (right): Keith Scott Morton
Page 79 (left): Gridley & Graves
Page 79 (right): Keith Scott Morton
Page 80 (top left): Keith Scott Morton
Page 80 (top middle): Robin Stubbert
Page 80 (top right): Michael Luppino

Page 80 (bottom): Michael Luppino
Page 81: Michael Luppino
Page 82 (left): Keith Scott Morton
Page 82 (right): Keith Scott Morton
Page 83 (left): Keith Scott Morton
Page 83 (right): Robin Stubbert
Page 84: Stacey Brandford
Page 86 (left): Gridley & Graves
Page 86 (right): Keith Scott Morton
Page 87 (all): William P. Steele
Page 88 (top): Keith Scott Morton
Page 88 (bottom): Keith Scott Morton
Page 89 (left): Keith Scott Morton
Page 89 (right): Keith Scott Morton
Page 90: Keith Scott Morton
Page 92 (left): Keith Scott Morton
Page 92 (right): Keith Scott Morton
Page 93: Keith Scott Morton
Page 94: Keith Scott Morton
Page 95: Keith Scott Morton
Pages 96–97: Keith Scott Morton
Page 98: Keith Scott Morton
Page 99: Keith Scott Morton
Page 100: Gridley & Graves
Page 102 (left): Keith Scott Morton
Page 102 (right): Keith Scott Morton
Page 103: Keith Scott Morton
Page 104 (left): Keith Scott Morton
Page 104 (right): Keith Scott Morton
Page 105 (left): Laura Resen
Page 105 (right): Stacey Brandford
Page 106: Michael Luppino
Page 107 (left): Grey Crawford
Page 107 (right): Keith Scott Morton
Page 108: Andrew McCaul and Catherine Gratwicke
Page 110: Keith Scott Morton
Page 111: Keith Scott Morton
Page 112 (left): Keith Scott Morton

# Index